Contents

Some words are shown in bold, **like this**. You can find them in the picture glossary on page 23.

What's awake?

Some animals are awake when you go to sleep.

Animals that stay awake at night are **nocturnal**.

What's

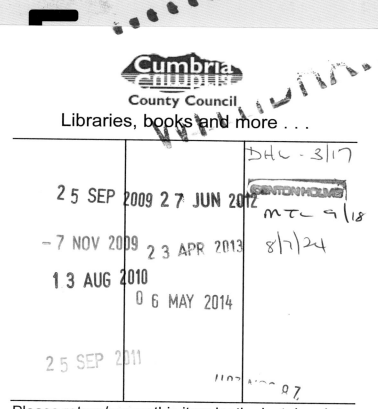

www.raintreepublishers.co.uk
Visit our website to find out more information about Raintree books.

To order:
☎ Phone +44 (0) 1865 888066
▤ Fax +44 (0) 1865 314091
▧ Visit www.raintreepublishers.co.uk

Raintree is an imprint of Capstone Global Library Limited, a company incorporated in England and Wales having its registered office at 7 Pilgrim Street, London, EC4V 6LB - Registered company number: 6695582

Edited by Adrian Vigliano and Diyan Leake
Designed by Joanna Hinton-Malivoire
Picture research by Tracy Cummins
Originated by Chroma Graphics (Overseas) Pte Ltd
Printed in China by South China Printing Company Ltd

ISBN 978 1 4062 1239 6 (hardback)
14 13 12 11 10
10 9 8 7 6 5 4 3 2 1

ISBN 978 1 4062 1244 0 (paperback)
14 13 12 11 10
10 9 8 7 6 5 4 3 2 1

British Library Cataloguing in Publication Data
Spilsbury, Louise
  Foxes. - 2nd ed. - (What's awake?)
  1. Foxes - Juvenile literature 2. Nocturnal animals - Juvenile literature
  I. Title
  599.7'75

Acknowledgements
We would like to thank the following for permission to reproduce photographs: Getty Images pp. **7** (© Don Johnston), **10** (© Jeff Foott), **14** (© Charles Krebs), **17** (© Peter Lilja); istockphoto pp. **4** (© paul kline), **6, 23a, 23b** (© Dmitry Deshevykh); Minden Pictures p. **15** (© John Hawkins); National Geographic Stock pp. **9** (© Norbert Rosing), **19** (© Rich Reid); Nature Picture Library p. **11** (© Warwick Sloss); Photolibrary pp. **8** (© Ronald Wittek), **13** (© AlaskaStock), **16** (© Tom Brakefield), **21** (© Imagesource Imagesource); Shutterstock pp. **5, 12** (© Yanik Chauvin), **18** (© Gert Ellstrom), **20** (© nialat), **22** (© Daniel Hebert), **23c** (© Martin Wall).

Cover photograph of a fox reproduced with permission of Capital Pictures (© Mel Longhurst). Back cover photograph of fur reproduced with permission of istockphoto (© Dmitry Deshevykh) and photograph of a fox's muzzle reproduced with permission of Shutterstock (© Daniel Hebert).

Every effort has been made to contact copyright holders of material reproduced in this book. Any omissions will be rectified in subsequent printings if notice is given to the publisher.

 CAUTION: Remind children that it is not a good idea to handle wild animals. Children should wash their hands with soap and water after they touch any animal.

Foxes are awake at night.

What are foxes?

Foxes are mammals.

Mammals have **fur** on their bodies.

Mammals live with their babies.

Mammal babies drink milk from their mother's body.

What do foxes look like?

Most foxes have orange-red **fur**.

They have black legs and white fur on their bellies.

muzzle

Foxes have big, bushy tails.

They have large, pointed ears and long **muzzles**.

Where do foxes live?

Some foxes live in woods.

Some live in hills or fields.

Foxes live where they can find food.

Sometimes they live near people.

What do foxes do at night?

Most foxes wake up just after dark.

Then they hunt for food.

Some foxes hunt all night.

Other foxes only hunt just after dark and before morning.

What do foxes eat?

In the wild, foxes usually eat rabbits, birds, and mice.

They sometimes eat plant roots and berries.

In the city, foxes eat these things, too.

They also eat food from rubbish bins or bird feeders.

What do foxes sound like?

Foxes can yelp and growl.

They may bark when they are angry.

Foxes call loudly to tell each other where they are.

They open their **muzzles** wide.

How are foxes special?

Foxes can hear very well with their big ears.

They can hear a tiny mouse squeak from far away.

Foxes can live in different places.

They can live near people or in the wild.

Where do foxes go during the day?

In the morning foxes find a safe place.

Then they lie down and go to sleep.

Sometimes foxes hunt during the day.

They do this if they cannot find food at night.

Fox map

tail

ear

muzzle

fur

Picture glossary

 **fur** soft hair that some animals have on their bodies

 **muzzle** nose and mouth of an animal such as a fox or dog

 **nocturnal** awake at night

Index

Note to parents and teachers

Reading for information is an important part of a child's literacy development. Learning begins with a question about something. Help the children think of themselves as investigators and researchers by encouraging their questions about the world around them. In this book, the animal is identified as a mammal. A mammal by definition is one that is covered with hair or fur, and feeds its young with milk from its body. Point out the fact that, although the animal in this book is a mammal, many other animals are mammals – including humans.

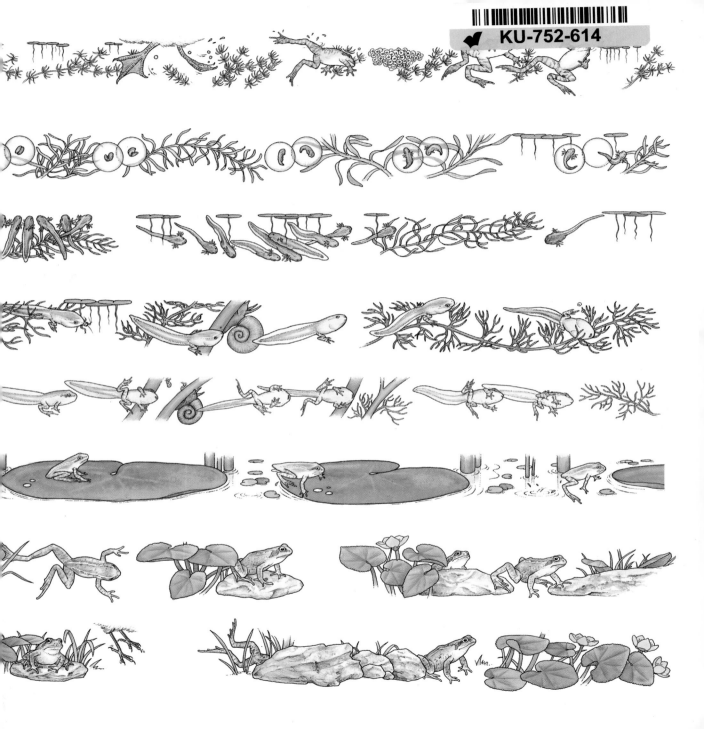

DK

A DORLING KINDERSLEY BOOK

Written and edited by Angela Royston
Art Editor Nigel Hazle
Production Marguerite Fenn
Illustrators Sandra Pond and Will Giles

Published in Great Britain by
Dorling Kindersley Limited
9 Henrietta Street, London WC2E 8PS

Paperback edition
2 4 6 8 10 9 7 5 3

A CIP catalogue record for this book is available
from the British Library

ISBN 0-7513-6626-9

Colour reproduction by Colourscan, Singapore
Printed in Singapore by Imago

SEE HOW THEY GROW

FROG

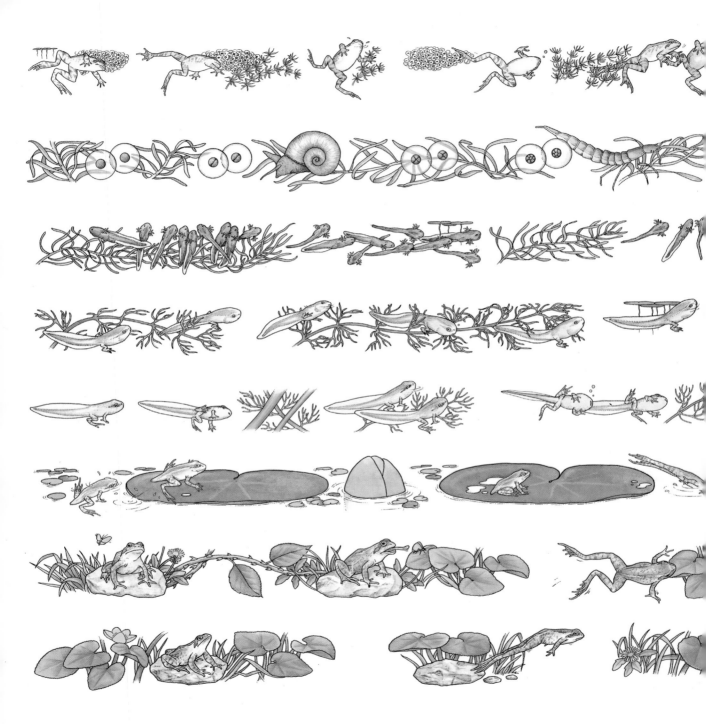

SEE HOW THEY GROW
FROG

photographed by
KIM TAYLOR
and JANE BURTON

DK

DORLING KINDERSLEY
London • New York • Moscow • Sydney

Growing in jelly

This frog is my mother. She has just laid all of these eggs in the water. The eggs are called frogspawn.